Original title:
The House of Forgotten Hopes

Copyright © 2025 Creative Arts Management OÜ
All rights reserved.

Author: Penelope Hawthorne
ISBN HARDBACK: 978-1-80587-118-7
ISBN PAPERBACK: 978-1-80587-588-8

Time's Unraveled Tapestry

In a corner sits an old shoe,
Holding dreams of a dance or two.
Yet it's stuffed with dust and a sock,
A relic of that wild clock's mock.

A teapot spills secrets in glee,
Whistling tales of a spoutless spree.
It brewed tea for one, not for two,
But still gets a chuckle, who knew?

The chair creaks tales of a cat's pride,
Who claimed its seat as a thrilling ride.
Now it's just a throne for a dust bunny,
Except for the times it hits the funny.

Postcards from places nobody went,
Picture-perfect smiles, all heaven-sent.
But the sender was lost in the mail,
Laughing at life's everlasting fail.

An old coat hangs with stories to tell,
Buttons missing, it knows all too well.
It dreams of dances and cozy nights,
Now it's only good for odd sights.

Echoes of Lives Unlived

Dusty shoes line the floor,
Whispers of adventures, wanting more.
A pirate hat on an old cat,
He thinks he's cool, but he's just fat.

Chasing dreams with a rubber band,
Building castles in the sand.
Forgotten toys, they giggle and sway,
In a world where the old folks play.

Nostalgia's Gritty Embrace

Pants too short, we danced like fools,
With soda pop and chocolate drools.
The record skips, a funny sound,
We spin around, fall to the ground.

In the attic, boxes stacked high,
Dust bunnies laughing, oh my, oh my!
With a sweater that smells like lost time,
Matching socks? Just a silly crime!

The Unraveling of Silent Heavy Hearts

Once I dreamed of flying high,
But tripped on clouds—my oh my!
With a pizza slice stuck in my hair,
I faced the world without a care.

Worn-out maps and crumpled plans,
A treasure hunt with just rubber bands.
The compass spins, so do I,
Maybe I'll just give it a try!

Charred Pages of Secret Stories

Once I wrote a tale of woe,
But spilled some juice, and now it's slow.
Ghosts of laughter fill the air,
With missing socks that just don't care.

Scrambled thoughts on crinkled sheets,
A chicken dance with two left feet.
Faded dreams and silly words,
Echo in forgotten herds.

Beneath the Dust, a Glimmer Glows

Beneath the dust, the socks do hide,
A pair long lost, with nowhere to bide.
Chasing dreams that once took flight,
Now tangled up in a sock's delight.

Once bright ideas, now faded gray,
They sneak around like a game of charades.
With laughter echoing through the halls,
As hope plays tag, and always falls.

Traces of Laughter Long Gone

Old chairs sway with a creaky song,
Remembering times where we'd all belong.
A tickle of joy in the air still stays,
Ghosts of giggles from yesterdays.

In the corners, a pillow fight's trace,
Furry friends hiding, can't keep their place.
The laughter hangs like cobwebs spun,
Wishing for battles, but the war is done.

Winds That Carry Old Wishes

The wind plays tricks with forgotten dreams,
Whispering tales of sunlit beams.
It tickles the curtains, a dance so sweet,
While nudging the snacks, stolen treats.

The garden gnomes nod with sly grins,
Plotting their heists on where to begin.
Sipping on wishes until they burst,
The neighbors complain, they're still the worst!

Through Forgotten Hallways We Wander

In hallways long and lined with lore,
We stumble upon an old, squeaky door.
Behind it lies a treasure trove,
Of dust bunnies planning their next move.

With that, we giggle, hop to our feet,
As we dodge the fluffies near our feet.
The echoes of whispers fill our minds,
In this goofy realm where joy unwinds.

Fleeting Glimmers of Lost Ambitions

Once a dream, now a hat,
Lying flat where the cat sat.
Plans that danced on skies so blue,
Growled at by a sassy shoe.

Pies were baked in hopes so grand,
But ended up burnt, a crumbling band.
Chased my wishes down the lane,
Found a squirrel, he took the blame.

Stars once twinkled in my brew,
Now they laugh in shades of dew.
A garden sprouted dreams divine,
But weeds showed up, declared them mine.

So sip the tea, let out a snort,
Ambitions fade, but oh, what sport!
With laughter echoing through the air,
Lost hopes bring joy, beyond compare.

The Eyes that Watch in Silence

Behind the curtain, they all stare,
Peeking at my old green chair.
Eyes like saucers, round and wide,
Who knew they'd be my silent guide?

They've seen my hair in crazy styles,
And trials met with quirky smiles.
Gazing down from dusty shelves,
I catch them whispering to themselves.

The goldfish thinks he rules this place,
With bubble thoughts that make no trace.
While clocks tick loudly with a grin,
Saying, 'Time to start again!'

So here's to watchers, quiet and sly,
Who giggle gently when I sigh.
From silly dreams to stumbles bold,
They keep my secrets, safe and old.

Threads of Memory in Tangled Light

I strung my hopes on shoelaces tight,
Climbed a tree to reach some light.
But falling down with quite a thud,
Left me tangled in a puddle of mud.

A sock once carried all my dreams,
Washed away in bubbly streams.
Now it dangles from a cloudy drip,
Taunting me with every trip.

Sunlight caught in vintage frames,
Whispers soft of old-time games.
My memories dance, but get lost fast,
Riding the waves of a clumsy past.

So spin a tale, give it a shake,
With every twist, a new mistake.
In tangled threads, life does delight,
And memories bloom in strings of light.

Castles Made of Wishes

With sand and dreams, I build so tall,
A castle big, I thought would sprawl.
But waves come crashing, take my time,
A sandy moat? Oh! What a crime.

Each grain a wish slipped through my hands,
Stuck with jellyfish and rubber bands.
I crown my work with a plastic king,
He wobbles proud with everything.

Not quite strong, but oh so bright,
Flickering candles in the night.
Even fallen, I'll laugh and cheer,
For each tiny castle, I hold dear.

So here's to dreams that ebb and flow,
With laughter wrapping me head to toe.
In every tumble, spark a grin,
For castles rise where hopes begin.

Dusty Corners of Longing

In a corner sat a shoe,
Its partner fled, who knew?
Longing for a pair so fine,
But trapped in webs of time.

A teapot sings an empty tune,
Waiting for a sunny noon.
Its lid is cracked, its spout is grim,
Still dreaming of the perfect whim.

A sandwich on the shelf could beam,
If only it could find its cream.
But mold has claimed this lunchtime jibe,
A relic from a past vibe.

The clock ticks loud but stands so still,
Baking dreams with a silent chill.
Laughter echoes, dust clouds form,
In the corners where hopes swarm.

Where Wishes Gather Dust

In a jar, a wish lies tight,
Scribbled dreams fade from sight.
Forgotten notes, a paper chase,
A dance of dust in empty space.

A rubber band can truly stretch,
But here it snaps, a tiny sketch.
Once a bouncy ball of cheer,
Now a joke that disappeared.

The broken toy sings lullabies,
To unfulfilled and endless sighs.
Its laughter echoes, once was bright,
Now it's just a ghost in flight.

Wishes wade in measures small,
That's how they end, after all.
The secrets that the walls have kept,
In the corners where they've slept.

Relics of Unspoken Promises

Underneath the creaky stair,
Lies a secret, dust with care.
A promise made with heartfelt giggles,
Now slips away, and slowly wriggles.

An old umbrella stands alone,
Poking fun with every groan.
Once it danced in rainy glee,
Now rusted jokes are its decree.

The doormat grins with half an eye,
A welcome mat that cannot lie.
It knows the stories of the past,
When all the laughter seemed to last.

Now, echoes linger, wrapped in dust,
Memories wane, but that's a must.
What once was bright has found a home,
In relics where forgotten roam.

Memories Stuck in the Wall

A photo stuck, askew with flair,
Shows joy, but now loves despair.
The smiles frozen with a wink,
A canvas where lost hopes sink.

A nail hangs on, just for fun,
Holding dreams that weigh a ton.
It juggles memories through the years,
While laughter flies, but sadness cheers.

The wallpaper peels in a sigh,
Whispering tales as days go by.
Stickers stuck with child-like craze,
Now add to this nostalgic haze.

Each crevice holds a tale or two,
Of dreams that spark but fade anew.
In the wall, the past is caught,
A funny dance that time forgot.

Canvas of Unfulfilled Visions

Once I painted dreams so bright,
Now they're just a funny sight.
A cat in boots, a fish in trees,
Who knew hope would be such a tease?

My easel wobbles, canvas asks,
Where's the courage, where's the sass?
A rainbow's pout, a cloud's lost fluff,
Turns out ambition just ain't enough.

I sketched a world with ice cream skies,
But it melted, oh what a surprise!
Each brushstroke drips with laughter's glee,
Lost within my own fantasy.

Laughter echoes, a polka-dot joke,
Each failed vision, a playful poke.
Yet I keep painting without a care,
For dreams are hilarious, if you dare!

Sunlight on Forgotten Paths

Oh look, the sun forgot to shine,
It tripped on shadows, how divine!
A squirrel's wearing my old flip-flops,
On this path where hope just hops.

Chasing sunlight, what a chase,
I fell right into a clown's embrace.
Balloons that floated, tangled in trees,
Who knew optimism was such a tease?

With each step, a giggle unfolds,
I swear, my shoe's got stories untold.
An adventure awaits, filled with chuckles,
Silly paths lead to laughter's chuckles!

So here I strut on these forgotten ways,
Tripping on rocks, and unplanned delays.
In this odd journey, hope's a prank,
Sunlight's laughter fills up the tank.

Cracks in the Foundation of Hope

There's a crack in the floor, it's shaped like a star,
My hopes tried to dance but fell from afar.
A foundation built on pancakes and pie,
Each wobble a reason for laughter nearby.

I put up a sign, 'Caution: Dreams crumbling!',
But in the chaos, I found joy rumbling.
Silly putty wishes, they squish and they stretch,
Through cracks of uncertainty, laughter's a fetch.

With each little ripple, a giggle appears,
As I joke with the walls, it cheers up my fears.
Each wobble's a reminder, I'm here to make fun,
In this house of humor, we all are the sun.

So let's dance on the cracks, the ground may just laugh,
And build from the chaos; it's a jubilant craft.
With hope in the cracks, let's all be absurd,
For joy's in the quirk, and laughter's the word!

The Last Light of Dimming Stars

The stars are yawning, the moon's lost its gig,
They say every twilight's an old magic jig.
A firefly's flicker, a comedic debate,
In this vast sky, I ponder my fate.

Stars whisper secrets of hopes gone awry,
A comet trips by, can you make him cry?
With laughter as fuel, I dream to outshine,
In dimming light, can humor align?

The last light fades, but I won't despair,
For shadows dance wildly, with none but a flare.
Each twinkle a chuckle, each wobble a cheer,
In this darkened sky, there's nothing to fear.

So let's toast to the dimming, with giggles so bright,
For every last sparkle brings laughter at night.
In the cosmic dance, may joy be our guide,
As stars stumble and fall, we'll laugh side by side!

The Attics of Trampled Hopes

In the attic, dust bunnies play,
Laughter echoes from yesterday.
Old toys dance in forgotten glee,
Whispers of how it used to be.

Underneath piles of musty old clothes,
Chicken hats and mismatched toes.
A jester's smile on a broken mask,
Yet no one there to fulfill the task.

A tuba lies next to a shattered dream,
Playing tunes of a dusty theme.
The grand piano can't keep its keys,
But the catji's still full of memories.

In this realm, ghosts trip on their feet,
Trying to make the memories sweet.
With a chuckle and a how-do-you-do,
They tumble back to the sky so blue.

Lullabies of Lost Futures

Once upon a time, dreams wore shoes,
Now they shuffle in colorful blues.
Hopping on clouds of marshmallow fluff,
Serenade hearts that've had enough.

Hiccups of laughter under the moon,
Echo with hopes that ended too soon.
A rubber chicken sings joyfully,
To lullabies of what used to be.

Delusions fed by a cupcake's glow,
The frosting's sweet and the sprinkles flow.
Yet frosting dreams can be quite absurd,
As we chase with glee, our hopes deferred.

In the corners, a teddy bears snore,
The lullabies sing of wanting more.
Yet joy resides in the still of night,
As lost futures giggle, taking flight.

Faded Pictures on the Mantel

Faded photos caught in a stare,
Laughter frozen, once filled the air.
Grandpa's wig now looks like a broom,
Granny's wild dance? A practiced loom.

In frames of wood chipped and shy,
A cat in a hat passes by.
Each snapshot whispers tales of delight,
Of birthdays, cupcakes, and endless night.

Confetti clings to memories held,
While a rubber ducky quietly yelled.
Silly moments captured just so,
Like spaghetti jokes that steal the show.

Yet behind the glass, smiles fade away,
Hoping to giggle another day.
But laughter's the glue that holds tight,
In faded pictures, memories ignite.

The Unseen Gallery of Ambitions

In a gallery where dreams are shy,
Painted aspirations wave goodbye.
Pasta dressed like a grand old king,
  Bow ties made of leftover string.

Sculptures made from yesterday's news,
Brush strokes mixed in mustard hues.
Each canvas tells a tale of woe,
Yet tickles with each twist and blow.

Favor the quirks, let laughter lift,
A clown shoes are the perfect gift.
In this gallery of whimsical cheer,
  Hope wears a tutu, oh so near.

With each display, ambitions blend,
A funny twist at each sharp bend.
The unseen dreams dance in delight,
  In this gallery, we take flight.

Reveries We Left Behind

Dust bunnies dance on the floor,
While memories kick open the door.
Leftovers from dreams we won't claim,
Eating snacks in a wild, silly game.

Chairs throw shade on the walls,
As the laughter gives way to soft calls.
Tickling the clock with a joke,
Ignoring the echoes of things we broke.

In the Shadow of Abandoned Dreams

A couch wears a cape like a hero,
Draped in old popcorn and zeroes.
Who knew that silence was so loud?
As forgotten hopes draw a crowd.

Tangled up in a rug's embrace,
We discover a long-lost racing place.
The fridge hums songs from yesterday,
While we argue about who'll win at play.

The Heartbeat of a Forgotten Season

Socks covered in dust play hide and seek,
Joking about how they feel weak.
A calendar smiles with doodles,
Reminders of life's little poodles.

In a corner, a stack of old mail,
Whispers stories of a fantastic tale.
With each flip, we just might find,
A treasure of laughs left behind.

Stationary Stories of the Silent

A chair with a hat just sits and grins,
Experiencing the ups and downs of spins.
Giggles trapped in forgotten seams,
Sharing secrets of long-lost dreams.

Fruits in bowls for decades have chill,
Plotting mischief up on the windowsill.
They all know the punchline too well,
Hoping one day they'll break out of shell.

Reflections in a Dusty Mirror

In a room where dreams decay,
Dust bunnies dance and play.
Mirrors laugh, show old grins,
'Is that your face? Where you been?'

Old shoes hang like ghosts of flair,
Did I wear them? No, I swear!
Each reflection tells a joke,
I burst out laughing, then I choke.

Balancing my hopes on a chair,
It creaks loudly, I gasp for air.
A sandwich crust just rolled on by,
Pretend it's art, oh me, oh my!

In this place of lost delights,
Where laughter echoes through the nights.
I'll grab a broom, sweep dreams away,
But first, let's all just laugh and stay!

Unraveled Threads of Belief

One sock missing, the other here,
Do they conspire? So unclear.
The universe has jokes to tell,
Maybe socks have wished me well?

Yarn and wishes, tangled fine,
Turns out, crochet is not divine!
Grandma's lessons float like air,
Yet my knitting dreams go nowhere.

An old hat pops out—what's its fate?
Turns out it's just a dust plate!
With every stitch and every sigh,
I knit my quirks as days go by.

Threads of laughter, frayed and bold,
Stories of yarn that never told.
Beliefs unravel, but I will weave,
A tapestry—what can I believe?

Silhouettes of Silent Yearning

Shadows peek from behind the door,
Hoping for laughter, wanting more.
A cat on the sill, tail a wave,
Whispers secrets, oh how brave!

Chairs pose, like they're in the know,
"Who's coming?" they ask, putting on a show.
Forgotten hats gather in a pile,
When you stop by, they'll wear a smile!

Pictures frame a life once bright,
With faces laughing, oh what a sight!
Yet here we sit, shadows at play,
In a world that's lost its way.

Silhouettes dance in the moon's soft glow,
Winking at starlight—'Where will we go?'
Yearning for days with a quirky twist,
Laughter in silence, how could we resist?

The Unopened Letter

A letter waits, but what's the fuss?
It giggles away, like 'Who'll discuss?'
Worn-out stamps with tales half told,
A time machine, if you're bold.

Inside it's filled with frozen cheer,
Thoughts of me, and pizza beer.
In this mailbox of dreams untamed,
I wonder if I'll be blamed?

Maybe it's from a friend gone wild,
With jokes and riddles, and woes compiled.
Holding on to each little zing,
A time-bomb of words, ready to spring!

So I keep it closed, just for fun,
Imagining laughter when it's done.
When the moment's right, I'll read the tale,
Until then, let the silence prevail.

Melancholy in Every Corner

In the attic, dust bunnies play,
Whispering secrets of yesterday.
A broken chair sighs with glee,
While echoes of laughter cling to the spree.

The fridge hums a tune, quite out of key,
Refrigerated dreams of what used to be.
Old socks dance to the laundry's despair,
Unmatched and jolly, floating in mid-air.

A cat on the windowsill, plotting her stealth,
While a spider spins webs with utmost health.
They giggle at narratives, they'll never share,
In the most peculiar of lost places, beware!

Each creak tells a tale of mischief anew,
Of hiccups at parties where no one knew.
With puddles of memories, the floorboards quip,
Their stories tumble out, on a whimsical trip.

Tales of What Lies Beneath

Beneath the floorboards, lost socks do stir,
They've formed a rebellion, causing a blur.
With tales of adventures past laundry days,
Conspiring against their human's malaise.

The dust in the corner wore a tiny hat,
Claiming it conquered a mouse, or a rat.
A coat hanger hung low, like he was a king,
With dreams of a valiant coat-covering fling!

Here lies a sandwich, with mold as a cap,
Wishing for freedom in a magical map.
He dreams of a picnic, with sky and soft grass,
But instead, he's a legend, long gone with the class.

Crayons debate whether red's better than blue,
In crayon kingdoms where colors ensue.
They scribble and laugh, unbothered by fate,
Painting rainbows in the atmosphere—quite great!

Reflections on the Shattered Glass

Once a mirror, now just shards,
Reflecting the chaos of our backyard cards.
Each piece of glass, a smile or a frown,
Aggravated giggles in a lighthearted gown.

The winds whisper secrets, quite hard to hear,
Of romances passed, of laughter and cheer.
Bubbles of hope float like a drunken fairy,
While the dust motes pirouette, none too wary.

The clock ticks loudly, but no one does care,
In a world where time's quite simply unfair.
It holds little grudges on coffee-stained nights,
While the curtains waltz in the soft moonlight fights.

One last reflection in cracked fame and glory,
Of tales that don't end, and rather just hoary.
A scene of delight, in fragments it pours,
Leaving giggles lingering behind the closed doors.

The Weight of Unvoiced Sorrows

A shoe upon the shelf, feeling quite blue,
Wonders if freedom would fit him anew.
With laces to tie and stories to share,
He dreams of the sidewalks, waiting in despair.

A rogue pencil rolls, craving a page,
To scribble a tale of humor and rage.
He taps on a notebook, begging for fate,
While being ignored, he begins to create.

The old clock sighs, swinging 'round and 'round,
Its tick-tocking laughter is the best sound.
But watch out, dear friend, for the first break of dawn,
The sun spills its sunshine, and the dreams are all gone!

A curtain droops low, feeling quite shy,
Whispering tales to the birds in the sky.
They listen and chirp, in tunes rather sappy,
While the weight of the world feels a touch too flappy.

Lost Tales of the Unseen

In shadows where laughter used to reside,
A dog in a hat tries his best to hide.
Old wishes in corners, they gather like dust,
While a cat plays the piano, it's quite a must.

The fridge talks at midnight, a true gourmet,
Reciting old recipes in a cheeky way.
A sock puppet knight guards the door with a grin,
His sword made of yarn, let the silliness begin!

Chairs hold meetings, discussing their fate,
While tables try to negotiate dinner plate.
Bottles of ketchup argue over the shelf,
Claiming they're better when served by themselves.

The clock strikes a joke, then starts to unwind,
Tickling the moments we'd rather not find.
Here lies the humor in hopes left to roam,
In a place marked by laughter we call it our home.

Dim Light in the Empty

A bulb flickers gently, winking in jest,
Shadows dance, twirling, they're having a fest.
The old couch just sighed, it's tired of the wait,
As dust bunnies gossip 'bout love at first rate.

A ghost in the corner is knitting a scarf,
For a spine-chilling cat who refuses to laugh.
The window's a bracket for stories gone wrong,
While curtains join in, humming a song.

An echo of giggles hangs over the hall,
Remnants of parties that could have been small.
Framed pictures high up roll their eyes in disdain,
Wondering if anyone remembers their names.

The fridge hums a tune, like a rock and roll star,
While leftovers grumble, "We've not come so far."
In corners so deep, with a sigh and a glance,
Hope stumbles and giggles, waiting to dance.

Guardians of Forgotten Dreams

A broom rides the night on a whimsical quest,
To sweep up the dreams that used to be best.
With each little swoosh, it chuckles along,
Collecting the wishes, a raucous old song.

The mirror reflects what it chooses to see,
A fish in a tuxedo, grinning with glee.
While pillows conspire to fluff up the truth,
Tales of wild adventures from the days of youth.

A teddy bears' summit holds secrets in threads,
Discussing the nightmares by cutting off heads.
Left slippers giggle, their dance is in sight,
As the dust settles slowly, preparing for flight.

The moon winks a smile, it's quite a good sport,
As the shadows engage in their nightly court.
In a space of lost dreams and giggles so grand,
Hope plays the jester, creating a brand.

The Color of Forgotten Wishes

A paintbrush forgotten, with colors so bright,
Dabs of old laughter paint shadows at night.
With strokes full of whimsy, it colors the past,
Bringing forth wishes that faded too fast.

Old crayon philosophers preach in the drawer,
About dreams made of filling and tales to explore.
The purple one mutters, "I wish we were free,
To color the world, oh how fun it would be!"

Meanwhile, the walls sigh, full of stories and scenes,
Of fairy tale moments and glittery dreams.
A rug attempts mindfulness, twisting its fate,
In hopes that the joy can rejuvenate.

Pumpkins play saxophones, midnight's delight,
While raindrops join hands to twirl in the night.
In this carnival space, where silliness tries,
Hope juggles its laughter, in a rainbowed disguise.

Through the Veil of Time

In a corner, lost and meek,
A sock claims to hide a peak.
It laughs at all the shoes that roam,
Whispering tales of a comfy home.

A dust bunny wears a tiny hat,
Conspiring with the old family cat.
They plot to steal a juicy bite,
Of crumbs that danced away from sight.

The coffee pot has dreams at night,
Of brewing up a future bright.
But all it gets is cold and still,
While mugs all envy a bachelor's fill.

Yet in this chaos, giggles rise,
From hidden toys in clever guise.
With every creak and every squeak,
Lost hopes chuckle, oh so chic.

The Secrets Held by Shadows

In the hallway, shadows creep,
Trading secrets, oh so deep.
A whisper from the old broomstick,
Jokes about a ghostly trick.

The curtains twitch, they want to play,
With sunlight bending in a fray.
They giggle with the dust motes free,
Plotting pranks on old Aunt Bee.

Hidden behind the mystery's veil,
A rubber chicken tells a tale.
It shares its story, filled with laughter,
Chasing gloom away, ever after.

So raise a toast to shadows' guile,
As they dance and twist awhile.
In their laughter, a truth we find,
That joy can linger, unconfined.

Echoes of the Unsung

In the attic, quiet and tight,
A ukulele plays at night.
It strums the dreams of folks long gone,
While dust collects on old bobbleheads' dawn.

A picture frame starts to grin,
Singing tunes of where it's been.
Neighbors' rumors toss and spin,
About the lives that once had been.

Old stories float on gentle breeze,
Pants that lost their way with ease.
The echoes laugh, a joyful reign,
Turning memory into sweet champagne.

So gather 'round, both young and old,
For tales that never will grow cold.
In laughter's warmth, all hearts will cling,
To unsung joys that memories bring.

In the Quiet We Find

Beneath the stair, a treasure lies,
A broken toy with hopeful eyes.
It dreams of fields far and wide,
Finding friends that won't subside.

The teapot hums a gentle tune,
As sunlight spills like dreams in June.
It chuckles softly, no reason for gloom,
While every sigh begins to bloom.

Old shoes sit tight, their leather worn,
Recalling dances they have sworn.
They tap a beat, inspiring glee,
Reminding all of who we could be.

In these whispers, the joy unwinds,
For in the quiet, laughter binds.
With every chuckle, hopes arise,
Finding solace in the guise.

Echoing Wishes in the Void

In a room where dreams did wait,
A cat plays chess, it's far too late.
The goldfish judges, floating high,
While curtains wave a ghostly bye.

Old wishes hang like dusty clothes,
A dancing ghost with silly toes.
The clock insists on ticking loud,
While crickets join the laughing crowd.

In every corner, echoes chuckle,
As lost ambitions start to shuffle.
A rubber plant sings out of tune,
While shadows play a merry rune.

Yet hope runs wild in silly styles,
It wears a hat, it grins and smiles.
Amongst the clutter, joy persists,
In this strange realm where nothing's missed.

Resilient Whispers of the Past

In the attic, tales unwind,
Where mismatched socks and ghosts are kind.
An old board game, so forlorn,
Plays tricks on all who try to mourn.

Cobwebs dance with stories old,
Each whisper wrapped in secret gold.
An echo of a lost balloon,
That floated off to chase the moon.

Tickling dust makes giggles rise,
As memories wear their silly ties.
A box of crayons, bent but bright,
Draws doodles on the walls of night.

Yet in this jumble, laughter stays,
As every moment finds its ways.
Resilient dreams in crooked frames,
Poke fun at life, and mock its games.

Flickering Flames of Lost Cherished Moments

A candle flickers, whispers low,
Playing tag with shadows that flow.
It spouts some jokes, though quite bizarre,
You never know just where they are.

A photograph, with smudged effects,
Remembers laughter and some defects.
The family parrot, wise and gray,
Keeps secrets safe and curls in play.

Moments danced on threads of time,
Each one a riddle, each a rhyme.
With every flick, a grin ignites,
As dreams pretend to reach new heights.

Yet in the glow of memory's loom,
Sweet echoes chase away the gloom.
For what was lost comes back anew,
In giggles soft, in warmish hue.

Forgotten Corners of the Mind

In the attic of my cluttered mind,
Old thoughts are frayed, they're mostly blind.
A forgotten sock, a puzzling riddle,
Dances to its own weird fiddle.

In every crevice, dreams lay low,
Bouncing back with each toe-toe.
The toaster sings a jolly tune,
While spoons debate what time is noon.

Muffled giggles from faded schemes,
Bring forth the fruit of jumbled dreams.
Past plans slide in a zealous twirl,
As marbles roll and hope does swirl.

Yet in this maze of whimsy bright,
Resides a spark, a playful light.
For every corner breathes a giggle,
In this strange place where thoughts just wiggle.

Weeds in the Garden of Dreams

Roses spoke to daisies warm,
While weeds debated their sly charm.
They plotted glee beneath the sun,
Their leafy laughter, oh what fun!

Daffodils danced, but roots did shake,
As clovers giggled, "What a mistake!"
With dreams so bright, they found their way,
To wiggle and waddle through the day.

One lost a shoe, the other a hat,
While snails took bets on who was fat.
In each tiny sprout a secret lay,
Of whimsical hopes that ran astray.

Though gardeners frowned and pulled their best,
The weeds just chuckled, "We're the jest!"
For in this chaos, laughter blooms,
And wild ambitions fill all rooms.

The Last Echo of Forgotten Whispers

In corners where the dust bunnies sleep,
Old whispers gather, secrets they keep.
They chuckle softly, share silly tales,
Of paper boats and old ginger ales.

A sock fell lost, it spoke with pride,
"I've been on adventures, come take a ride!"
They laughed at the mice, those tiny thieves,
Who always stole crumbs, among the leaves.

The clock chimed loud, a quirky tune,
While shadows danced under the moon.
Each tick a treasure, each tock a cheer,
For echoes of nonsense drifted near.

In this old room, no whispers of dread,
Just laughter of things left unsaid.
The past is a jester, with stories to spin,
Inviting us all to join in the grin.

Whispers in Abandoned Rooms

In the attic, where old chairs creak,
Whispers of mischief giggle and sneak.
They play hide and seek 'neath dust bunnies' eyes,
Swapping stories of pies and surprise.

A hat that tiptoed, and shoes that laughed,
In shadows they plotted, each prank half crafted.
The window, a stage for a moth in flight,
While laughter echoed into the night.

They spoke of a cat, who once wore a crown,
But royal affairs made him tumble down.
The lampshade snickered with bits of dust,
In this grand palace, they all play just.

For every corner, a giggle haunts,
A chair that wobbles, a curtain that taunts.
In abandoned spaces, where spirits roam,
It's a raucous party, come grab a dome.

Echoes of Unclaimed Dreams

Beneath the moon, lost dreams took flight,
With echoes of laughter that sparkled bright.
They tangled their hopes in misfit schemes,
Strutting in jest through impossible dreams.

A firefly sparkled, "I'm a star tonight!"
While daydreams danced in pure delight.
A kite that tangled with laundry's grasp,
Said, "Catch me if you can!" with a playful gasp.

Unclaimed wishes rode a wild breeze,
Tickling the trees, as playful as tease.
They swirled 'round the lamp, making shadows play,
In this whimsical world, they wittily sway.

So gather your wishes, let laughter gleam,
For echoes surround us, chasing a dream.
In the heart of the night, let joy take its flight,
With echoes of humor, everything's right.

Fragments of Distant Tomorrows

In a cupboard stacked with old good cheer,
Dust bunnies dance like they own the year.
Forgotten plans hang on rusty hooks,
While spaghetti monsters lurk in dusty books.

Leftover dreams have turned to potpourri,
Chasing rainbows on a broken spree.
The calendar's pages tick in slow motion,
As socks argue about their socky devotion.

Whispers of laughter echo through the hall,
As time plays tricks, and shadows fall.
A corncob pipe adorns a faded throne,
Where old hopes gather and live with a groan.

In pajamas of past, they waltz through the haze,
With giddy thoughts of improbable praise.
Each chuckle a memory of what could be,
In this silly realm of what never will be.

Ghosts of Desires Lost

In the attic, dreams play hide and seek,
One sighs loudly, another just squeaks.
Old wishes live on dusty shelves,
Surrounded by taxidermied elves.

Popcorn ceilings whisper stories untold,
As aspirations turn a bit too bold.
An avocado toast dreams of being gourmet,
While reality serves it on a dull tray.

Invisible friends host a jubilee,
Juggling deadlines with glee and esprit.
They sip on the nectar of sweet, sweet regret,
Laughing at plans no one would ever fret.

Unicorns prance around a broken clock,
Ticking laughter, like a ticklish sock.
Each tick-tock remixes what we once sought,
In this grand show of whimsical thought.

The Quiet Garden of Dreams

In a garden where sunlight was shy,
Fairy tales grow on a pumpkin pie.
A snail with ambitions takes a slow ride,
While daisies giggle, swaying with pride.

Petunias peak, wearing polka dots bright,
Planning a ball that starts at midnight.
The hedgehog conducts a symphony bold,
As whispers of wishes turn to stories told.

Clouds float by in a dreamy parade,
As cacti debate the best way to fade.
One claims it's grand to live in the thorn,
While tulips just snicker, forever reborn.

With butterflies plotting a mischief or two,
They sprinkle the moments with laughter anew.
This quiet garden thrives on delight,
Where hope takes a nap and dreams take flight.

Veils Over Past Ambitions

Behind curtains made of frayed aspirations,
Echoes of laughter spark wild interpretations.
A pinball machine of hopes long forgotten,
Plays tunes of triumph that seem quite rotten.

In this realm where the clock's not a friend,
Gumdrops and giggles never seem to end.
Old charts map dreams that turned to balloon,
Drifting away like a misplayed tune.

The blender croons songs of yesterday's scheme,
Whipped up delights in a frothy dream.
With sprinkles of joy and a dash of regret,
Life's quirky buffet—don't forget your pet!

So we tiptoe past these potential regrets,
While cats in bowties throw lavish duets.
Veils flutter softly, revealing the show,
Of whimsy and laughter that endlessly flow.

Shadows of Long-Lost Aspirations

Once a dreamer walked with pride,
Now they trip over thoughts they hide.
Old ambitions gather dust, you see,
Like socks beneath the mystery tree.

Plans for riches once drawn in chalk,
Turn to giggles during evening walk.
Laughter fills the rooms of dread,
As visions dance like an old marionette.

In the attic lies a time machine,
But all it does is make me keen.
Chasing whispers of misspent days,
While dust bunnies join in the play.

So here I sit with hope on a throne,
Building castles from dreams overgrown.
Who knew the past could be this ludicrous?
In shadows, I still find joy, ridiculous.

Remnants of Yesterday's Visions

Once bright ideas hang like pegs,
Now they wobble on two wooden legs.
Sketches made in a hurry and haste,
Have morphed into a curious waste.

I planned to fly, but here I stand,
With a collection of rocks in hand.
Each stone a hope that I could lift,
Yet they're smarter and do the drift.

"Tomorrow," I said, "I'll make a start,"
Yet here we are, with half a heart.
Laundry piles sing their forlorn songs,
While optimism prances along.

But who needs dreams that climb so high?
When life's more fun with a wobbly pie.
We'll feast on laughter, but not on toast,
As remnants swirl, a delightful ghost.

Silence Among Dusty Corners

Beneath the stairs, where echoes rest,
Lurks an ambition that never confessed.
It whispers, "Hey, remember me?"
While I swear it's Netflix on free spree.

Cobwebs hang like covers on tales,
Of woozy hopes and grand-fail gales.
Polite giggles from the dusty gloom,
Inviting me to this shabby room.

Once I had plans, oh what a relief,
That turned into edible pantry thief.
I stood with a mop, ready to fight,
But it just laughed and said, "Not tonight!"

Instead I rest with a sandwich in hand,
Dreaming of trips to a far-off land.
Yet here I chuckle, with crumbs in my hair,
In corners where dreams like to hang out and stare.

Memories Linger on Empty Shelves

On shelves that creak with vibrant tales,
Rest dusty hopes in their quaint pails.
An abandoned trophy for a game I forgot,
Stands tall, yet it's just a forgotten plot.

Yesterday's battles bring fits of glee,
Like tripping over a cat or a tree.
Socks go missing in the quest for glory,
While laughter tells the best of the story.

Photos of fervor twitch in their frames,
Wink and nudge with whimsical names.
Each moment frozen, yet full of dance,
Inviting mischief with every glance.

So let's toast to dreams gone wild,
Like a spontaneous prank from a mischief child.
For who needs success when we can just smile,
On shelves where memories linger for a while.

Rusted Keys to Forgotten Futures

Old keys in a drawer, they jingle and laugh,
    Claiming to unlock a forgotten path.
They jiggle and shake, they promise a spree,
    But all they unlock is a memory of tea.

Once they belonged to a bike with a bell,
Now they're just trophies of cautionary tales.
The locks that they fit are a mystery still,
    Like finding a penny on top of a hill.

A treasure chest waits in the corner of gloom,
Filled with old socks, and a slight whiff of doom.
We can't find the gold, nor the riches they boast,
But I'll toast to the snacks that I find at the most.

Each rusted old key tells a tale to amuse,
Of escapades lost, and the paths we won't choose.
With a chuckle we throw them back into the fray,
    Spoon-feeding nostalgia with each silly sway.

Dreams Trapped Beneath Broken Beams

Beneath crooked rafters, where dreams tend to fester,
Lie the wishes of cats who were too vague to gesture.
They wanted to fly, and perhaps sip some cream,
Yet here they just nap, on a very odd dream.

Up in the attic, ghosts tickle your toes,
They giggle and snicker as reality doze.
Each beam overhead whispers hopes gone astray,
Like finding a shoe on a very odd day.

The moths dance in circles, plotting their flight,
Around crumpled letters from the past's funny plight.
"Dear future," they write, "I'll take mustard and jam!"
But it's hard to respond when you're stuck in a spam.

With dreams trapped in corners, and razors of light,
We laugh at their antics, like shadows in flight.
So let's raise a toast to the wishes so rare,
And let each broken beam be a chance to declare!

Echoing Lullabies of the Unremembered

In the shadows they linger, whispers take shape,
Where lullabies echo, in odd, twisted tape.
The tunes make you giggle, a whimsical sound,
Singing tales of the lost, as they twirl round and round.

Old slippers get cozy with rogue bits of fluff,
Waltzing through echoes, they're more than enough.
The stories they spin have been woven with care,
Like knitting a sweater for a pet monkey's hair.

Forgotten imaginations, dancing in moonlight,
They skip and they jump, with a curious flight.
The unremembered sing songs of delight,
As marbles and buttons take over the night.

We sway with the echoes, all giggles and glee,
In the embrace of the lullabies, wild and free.
So let's not forget this strange, merry sound,
Where the best of the past tumbles round and around.

Veils of Dust and Desire

Layers of dust, like a cake, they reside,
Veils of the past, with nowhere to hide.
They flutter and dance when the sunlight peeks in,
Making wishes for clean, in a way they can grin.

Like forgotten old toys, with a joke to bestow,
They whisper of childhood, and where did they go?
The plush bear insists that he still has a dream,
Of leading a parade of a most festive theme.

Hopes wrapped in cobwebs, a festival's glee,
Like trying to climb up a slippery tree.
The dust bunnies chuckle, as they tumble about,
Sharing secrets of joy, and what it's about.

So let's raise a glass to this whimsical state,
To dreams hidden deeply, but never too late.
In veils of dust, our laughter will shine,
Let's toast to the moments, both quirky and fine.

The Weight of Old Promises

In a corner, dreams are piled high,
Worn-out slippers and a lopsided tie,
A stack of wishes with dusty backs,
Held up by jokes and some old knickknacks.

Plans for fitness and fancy trips,
Now just whispers and playful quips,
The treadmill leans against the wall,
Dust bunnies laughing at our downfall.

Hopes once grand, now slightly worn,
Waltzing with regrets each dull morn,
Yet in the chaos, a chuckle brews,
Life's a circus; well, what's the use?

Underneath it all, laughter stays,
Silly motifs in these cluttered bays,
Still dreaming dreams in mismatched socks,
Living life as a parody box.

Dusty Tomes of Lost Sentiments

Books stacked high with covers that fade,
Love letters penned but never relayed,
A diary filled with ice cream stains,
The ink like memories—slightly insane.

Once hopeful chapters of grand romance,
Now scribbled notes that barely dance,
Hearts and flowers lost in the fray,
Like old cartoonists gone astray.

Pondering how the plot could twist,
Each half-baked tale meets a hearty fist,
Back in the shelf where spirits lounge,
An epic saga of minor renown.

But laughs emerge from pages torn,
As stories flutter like clothes unworn,
Giggling dust motes in the midday sun,
Time resumes, and we just have fun.

Crumbling Walls of Resilience

Brick by brick, they threaten to fall,
Yet here we are, holding our all,
Walls that echo our foiled attempts,
Each crack a place for laughter's pretense.

"Perhaps a plant could spruce this up!"
We chuckle, ignoring the coffee cup,
Water leaks like a trickster's jest,
Yet here we gather, feeling our best.

Every flake of paint tells a joke,
Puns and giggles in hearty choke,
Still standing tall with a wobbly grin,
For life's a game we can always win.

Crumbling walls hold sturdy cheer,
Among the mischief, love steers clear,
A fortress of folly, laughter imbued,
Together we laugh, in this refuge renewed.

Sunlight Through the Gloom

Bright rays peek through a window pane,
Chasing shadows like a playful train,
Laughter bursts as beams collide,
Bouncing around, with nowhere to hide.

Dust motes dance in the golden light,
While our socks clash in a clothing fight,
A symphony of mismatched glee,
Who knew daylight would set us free?

Old curtains sway, with secrets in tow,
Whispers mingling with sunlight's glow,
Tickling fancies of unkempt dreams,
And we chuckle at our silly schemes.

In corners where gloom used to tread,
Joy flickers on like a fairytale thread,
Sunlit laughter, a charming plume,
Turns the ordinary into fun-filled zoom.

Wings of Hope that Once Soared

In a closet of wishes, they flutter about,
Unruly and cheeky, they laugh and they shout.
The dreams that were vibrant, they wiggle, they flip,
With socks that are missing, they plan a great trip.

They tried to play charades with a moldy old hat,
But the hat just kept snoozing, how rude of the brat!
With giggles and snickers, they danced in a line,
As the clock struck the hour, they whispered, "Not time!"

These figments of fun chase each other around,
With their wings made of paper, they leap and they bound.
But if you ask them, "Hey, where are you going?"
They'll just giggle and grin, then keep their wings glowing.

So gather your hopes, don't leave them alone,
In corners they frolic, they claim all they've grown.
With nothing but mirth, your smiles they will bring,
For those wings of great fantasy deserve to take wing.

Dreams Dispersed Like Leaves

A breeze blew through my worries one fine autumn day,
And scattered my dreams like kids on a fray.
They tumbled and twisted like leaves in the wind,
Each one with a story, a giggle, a spin.

One dream wore a hat made of peanut butter toast,
It danced with a pickle, and claimed it was host.
They laughed at the clouds as they juggled the sun,
"Oh, isn't life silly? We're just here for fun!"

In piles on the ground, my hopes made a mess,
A leaf blower came through, what a mental distress!
They whirled and they twirled, oh so hard to believe,
How laughter can sprout from dreams like those leaves.

But fear not, dear friend, it's a laugh riot, you see,
For these scattered dreams giggle with glee.
They'll rise once again, like more leaves in the air,
To dance in the wind—oh, just never despair!

Melodies of the Unremembered

Forgotten tunes linger like dust on the shelf,
They hum and they giggle, but never by self.
An old guitar grumbles, its strings tune awry,
With a wink and a nudge, it croons to the sky.

A cacophony swirls of sandwiches' cheer,
A anthem composed of the winks of a deer.
With veggies as backup, they form a parade,
Each note takes a bow, in the sun they cascade.

The tambourine jived with a polka-dot cat,
Old socks joined the rhythm, how wild and how fat!
Each beat offered laughter, no frowns to be found,
In the melodies past, joy spun all around.

So let's toast to the tunes that keep singing our name,
For the silliness crafted will never feel lame.
With rhythms unanchored, we dance down the lane,
To the melodies humored that never felt vain.

Reverberations of a Distant Past

In echoes of laughter from what was long gone,
The stories and mishaps still dance on the lawn.
With silly old pranks that the past tried to keep,
They twinkle like stars while we giggle and leap.

A time-traveling biscuit once claimed it was wise,
It ran from the oven, with sparkles in eyes.
"Who needs time machines?" it chuckled with glee,
"I'm here for the frosting, come share it with me!"

Old wishes nudge gently from corners and nooks,
Trading tales of adventure for forgotten old books.
They whisper, "Remember the fun we once had?"
As memories tickle the corners we've clad.

So here's to the echoes that bring back the cheer,
With laughter and jest, we'll hold them quite dear.
For moments once fleeting can dance back to play,
In this tapestry woven, let's celebrate sway!

Doors that Never Swing Open

There's a door with a sign that says 'Enter.'
But inside, it's a portrait of a toaster.
I knocked and I knocked, and I waited,
For a ghost of a sandwich to come out and boast her.

Invisible mice hold a dance on the stairs,
While the dust bunnies roll like they're in a parade.
The doorknob laughs as it plays with my cares,
In a world made of wishes that never get made.

A mailbox is filled with unbounded regret,
When the mailman forgot to deliver my cheer.
I tried to complain, but my voice was quite wet,
So I called on the cat, and it just disappeared.

If doors could laugh, this one would surely cry,
For the wishes it holds are as lost as my socks.
Yet I'll keep on knocking, and I'll never know why,
It's a circus of hopes with mismatched clocks.

Stains of Laughter on the Floor

In the corner, the carpet is weaving a tale,
Of spillages bright that once made us gleam.
A hiccup of joy on the surface so frail,
As we danced with the pudding, if pudding could beam.

There's a patch where the coffee had audibly cried,
While the juice took a tumble, all sticky and fun.
These stains tell the secrets of when we all tried,
To juggle the snacks and our dreams on the run.

I found a lost cookie underneath the cabinet,
A relic of laughter, a treasure we made.
It whispers of moments, a sugary habit,
While the vacuum of fate seems to have been waylaid.

So let's toast to the floor, with its canvas of joy,
For each drop was a burst of adventures we'd choose.
In our dance of mishaps, we find the alloy,
Of laughter and heartbeats, that we never lose.

The Twilight of Forgotten Dreams

As darkness creeps in, dreams do a jitter,
Twinkling like stars that forgot to be bright.
I caught one that whispered, "Oh please, don't you quit her,"
While the shadows all stumbled and tried to take flight.

In the corners, past wishes play games of charades,
With the echoes of hopes that jumped just too high.
But here comes a gopher, in kooky cascades,
And he zigzags around with a pie in the sky.

"Remember," it chuckles, "you once wanted ice cream?"
But alas, it's now biting each syllable's dust.
Still, we share every giggle and float on a beam,
As the twilight unveils the absurdity of lust.

So let's gather our dreams like confetti in air,
Sprinkle laughter on shadows, and prance through the night.
For in twilight's embrace, not a moment to spare,
We find joy in the dreams leaving behind their blight.

Chasing Shadows of What Could Have Been

A shadow once whispered, 'Let's play hide and seek,'
But I tripped on a memory and fell on my face.
It giggled and darted, with timing so sleek,
While I pondered the patience of this silly chase.

We rounded the bend where the hopes used to glow,
Near the wall with a map to nowhere at all.
I swear I just saw a dream put on a show,
Dressed in polka dots, ready to take its fall.

"Catch me if you can!" sang a thought from the past,
But my legs were too slow, and it danced like the breeze.
A tumble of wishes, all spooling so fast,
In a game of tag, where I'm always the tease.

Yet the shadows keep twirling, a whimsical game,
And I laugh at the wonders I never have seen.
Chasing my fantasies, wild and untamed,
In the corners of laughter, they sparkle and beam.

Faded Footsteps on Worn Floors

In a place where dreams went to snore,
Old slippers shuffle, nevermore.
Dust bunnies dance, a ragged crew,
They laugh at plans that never grew.

A cat naps on a half-eaten chair,
While ghosts of wishes float in the air.
We trip on laundry not put away,
Guess hope's taking a long holiday!

Echoes of the Unspoken Heart

Whispers linger, but they're quite shy,
Like a clown who forgot how to fly.
Hearts once spoke in loud, bold tones,
Now they're moping around like bored drones.

They peek from corners, rarely seen,
Waving flags of the might-have-been.
A serenade of what was planned,
Turns into a tuba made of sand.

Windows to What Could Have Been

Peering through the dusty glass,
I see a future that seems to pass.
There sits a chair where no one's been,
Gathering whispers of what could win.

The sun tickles these dreams so bright,
While pajamas hold a hope for flight.
Yet darts of reality poke the air,
As plans flop down like a lumpy chair.

Fragments of a Distant Tomorrow

Yesterday's hopes play peek-a-boo,
In a game that only they knew.
Procrastination wears a silly hat,
While dreams skitter around like a cat.

Crayon drawings on a faded wall,
Represent futures that never stood tall.
They chuckle softly, those plans of yore,
Playing hopscotch on a forgotten floor.

www.ingramcontent.com/pod-product-compliance
Lightning Source LLC
Chambersburg PA
CBHW062112280426
43661CB00086B/556